Bulldozers

By Jean Eick

The Child's World® Inc. ◆ Eden Prairie, Minnesota

Published by The Child's World®, Inc.
7081 W. 192 Ave.
Eden Prairie, MN 55346

Design and Production:
The Creative Spark, San Juan Capistrano, CA.

Photos: © 1998 David M. Budd Photography;
         p.11 © Jack Fields/Corbis

Library of Congress Cataloging-in-Publication Data
Eick, Jean, 1947-
         Bulldozers at work / by Jean Eick.
                 p. cm.
         Includes index.
         Summary: Explains what a bulldozer can do, how its different parts work, and how the opera-
tor manipulates it from inside the cab.
         ISBN 1-56766-525-X (lib. bdg. : alk. paper)
         1. Bulldozers--Juvenile literature. [1. Bulldozers.] I. Title.
TA725.E369 1998
624.1'52--dc21   98-13701
                                                                                    CIP
                                                                                    AC

Contents

On the Job

On the job, the bulldozer is a mighty machine. Instead of wheels, it has big **crawler tracks**. These big metal belts spin forward or backward to make the bulldozer move.

The bulldozer also has a huge **blade**

that crashes and bangs as it works.

The blade is a big, flat piece of metal
that is very strong.

The bulldozer's blade can push over trees. And its crawler tracks can crawl right over the fallen trees!

The blade can do other jobs, too.

It can flatten big piles of gravel to make

a new road.

Bulldozers are powerful enough to

climb very steep hills.

15

The **ripper** on the back of a bulldozer

is used to loosen rocks and concrete.

Then the blade can move them out
of the way.

Bulldozers move very slowly.

They are loaded onto big trucks

and moved from job to job.

Climb Aboard!

Would you like to see inside the **cab**?

Climb aboard! The bulldozer's driver is called the **operator**. The operator's cab sits up over the big crawler tracks. It has all the controls that make the bulldozer work. The operator uses pedals, levers, and sticks to move the bulldozer and its blade.

Up Close

1. The cab

2. The crawler tracks

3. The blade

4. The engine

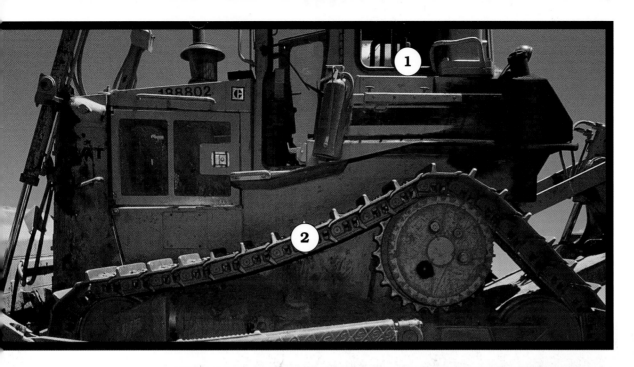

Glossary

blade (BLADE)
A bulldozer's blade is a big, flat piece of metal that can push, scrape, and dig.

cab (KAB)
A bulldozer's driver sits in a place called a cab. It has a seat and the pedals, levers, and sticks that control the bulldozer.

crawler tracks (KRAWL-er trax)
Crawler tracks are big metal belts that spin around to make the bulldozer move.
They can spin forward or backward.

operator (OP-er-ay-ter)
The operator is the person who drives the bulldozer and makes it work.

ripper (RIP-er)
The ripper is a strong metal arm on the back of a bulldozer. It moves up and down to loosen rocks and concrete so the bulldozer can move them more easily.